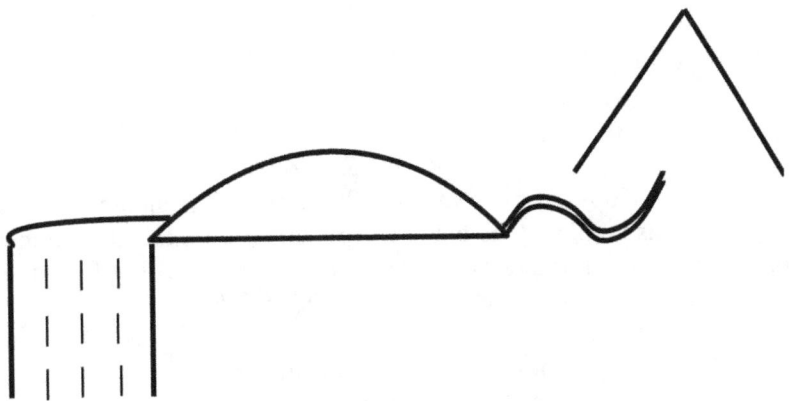

The American Accent Learnway™

Together, On the Road Inland

By

Adil Rehman, MA, MSHRM

All Rights Reserved.
Copyright © published 2022 by Adil Rehman.
No part of this book may be copied, replicated, reproduced, or transmitted
in any form or by any method or means without permission in writing from the copyright owner.
ISBN 979-8-9850855-2-5

For contact and other information,
please see the website: www.americanaccentlearnway.com

Disclaimer:
1. This Course does not state or imply that this Course is a substitute for Dictionaries or any particular Dictionary. It is an independent learning resource in the area of American English Pronunciation and Accent, and complements Dictionary content. Concurrent reference to Dictionary content is recommended.
2. For good reasons provided, this Course does not state or imply that the pronunciation given for word examples are identical with those provided by Dictionaries or any particular Dictionary. For an exact Dictionary pronunciation of any particular Dictionary, it is necessary to refer to that Dictionary.
3. In this Course, the Vocal Fidelity Phonetic System with its Accent sensitive features has been used to closely replicate Accent and pronunciation. Similarly, the content of the Four Lane Route, Vocal Pattern Tables, other Tables and explanation, provide guidance on Accent and Pronunciation. Following a scientific approach toward the development of knowledge, all of these are presented in a manner that is transparent that can be independently tested. No guarantee is offered, nor liability accepted in case of any error.

Contents.

Copyright © published 2022 by Adil Rehman.

Chapter 1:
Note On Prior Reading Required.

It is necessary to read Coursebook One "The American Accent Learnway™ – Cross the Bridge, Over the Divide" before beginning Coursebook Two, "The American Accent Learnway™ – Together, On the Road Inland". Coursebook One should be available with you for reference, as needed, as you go through Coursebook Two.

As a reminder, Coursebook One contains:

  -the Four Lane Route,
  -the complete introduction to Vocal Patterns,
  -the Appendices that elaborate the Vocal Fidelity Phonetic System,
  -the Appendix with the Table: Vocalizing Words With Irregular Vowel-Consonant Sequences, which you.
  may need to refer to from time to time.

The above constitute the knowledge foundation that enable a full understanding of the Vocal Pattern Tables, one presented in each of the three Coursebooks.

In addition, Coursebook One also contains:

  -the most common words pronounced the American way, and
  -words that are differently used by Americans, and finally,
  -the Vocal Pattern Bridge Table with the most Distinctive Vocal Patterns, accompanied by corresponding Word List Tables for selected Vocal Patterns from this table.

The present Coursebook Two, as follows here, contains the Vocal Pattern Inland Table with very Distinctive Vocal Patterns. This is accompanied by Word List Tables for selected Vocal Patterns from this table.

Coursebook Three follows as the sequel to the current Coursebook. It contains the Vocal Pattern Summit Table with clearly Distinctive Vocal Patterns. With this, the corresponding Word List Tables for selected Vocal Patterns from this table are provided.

Chapter 2:
The Vocal Pattern Road Inland.

The Vocal Pattern Road Inland follows after the Vocal Pattern Bridge, on the American Accent Learnway™. I abbreviate the name of the Vocal Pattern Road Inland, by leaving out "Road", when referring to the Vocal Pattern Table it contains. It is always therefore referred to as the Vocal Pattern Inland Table and not the Vocal Pattern Road Inland Table. This Table contains very Distinctive Vocal Patterns, in contrast with the Vocal Pattern Bridge Table which contains the most Distinctive Vocal Patterns. It precedes the Vocal Pattern Summit Table which covers clearly Distinctive Vocal Patterns.

Table:
The Vocal Pattern Inland Table

Note 1: The Notes for this Table apply to all the Vocal Pattern Tables, i.e. the Vocal Pattern Bridge Table, the Vocal Pattern Inland Table and the Vocal Pattern Summit Table. They provide essential explanation, about Vocal Patterns, to understand these Tables. They also explain the contents of the different columns.
Note 2: The "Vocal Pattern" in this Course has been defined as a recurring sound sequence, beginning with a Vowel and ending with a Consonant, heard in different words. Vocal Patterns are identified in the column headed "Vocal Pattern Name" (Column 2).
Note 3: Fundamentally different vocalizations of a particular Vocal Pattern that like all Vocal Patterns recur across words are called Vocal Pattern Variants. When a Vocal Pattern has Variants, each is considered a separate Vocal pattern and is listed in a separate row in the Vocal Pattern Name column with an identifying Roman numeral extension (Column 2). The name of the Vocal Pattern or Vocal Pattern Variant is the Vowel-Consonant Sequence of which it is composed, and the Roman numeral extension, if any. E.g. the Vocal Pattern 'IN' has several different Variants, e.g., as in the words "Grin", and "Line", which are Variants 'I' and 'II' respectively. These Variants are represented 'IN - I' and 'IN - II', in the "Vocal Pattern Name" column. Variants may be in Different Vocal Pattern Tables, i.e. the Vocal Pattern Bridge, Inland or Summit Tables. (Vocal Patterns of Insignificant Distinctiveness are identified only in the Vocal Pattern Master Table.) When a Roman numeral extension is seen as part of a Vocal Pattern name, in the "Vocal Pattern Name" column, it means that other Variants for that Vocal Pattern exist. To check the vocalization of a particular word which contains a Vocal Pattern that has many Variants, look for the Variant with word examples that are similar, in the "Word Example" column (Column 8) in the rows corresponding with the different Vocal Pattern Variants. A word with a Vowel-Consonant Sequence which has a unique or near unique vocalization is considered an Irregular vocalization and is not included as a Vocal Pattern Variant. E.g. the Vocal Pattern letter sequence 'AN' in the word "Orange" is often vocalized {O-ra*(i)*nge} with the 'A' Silent and replaced with an 'I' Soft sound. This is an Irregular example of this Vowel-Consonant Sequence. Except for a similar sound in the plural of the word, i.e. "Oranges", it is hard to find another word where 'AN' is so vocalized. This is therefore considered an Irregular vocalization of 'AN' and is not included as a Variant of 'AN' Vocal Patterns. (It should be noted that "Orange is also often vocalized {O-ra*(i1)*nge} with an 'I' Short – instead of the 'I' Soft, which is not an Irregular vocalization.)

Note 4: Vocal Patterns that begin with Vowel(s) in common but end with a different Consonant thus sharing a similar initial Vowel Sound have often been grouped together as a "Vocal Pattern Family". A Vocal Pattern Family can be recognized from the Variable Consonant Symbol '^' substituting the place of a final specific Consonant Sound.

> E.g. the Vocal Pattern 'OUN' as heard in the word "Count", has a similar initial Vowel Sound as the Vocal Pattern 'OUD' as heard in the word "Cloud". These related Vocal Patterns may be shown under one Vocal Pattern Family by joining the common preceding Vowels with the Variable Consonant Symbol '^' as in 'OU^'. This method is used to include 'OUD', 'OUN', 'OUT', etc. in one Vocal Pattern Family.

The Variable Consonant Symbol '^' applies to any Consonant which when Linked with common immediately preceding Vowels, produces a similar Vocal Pattern vocalization differentiated only by the different End Consonant Sound, such as is illustrated by examples in the "Word Example" column.

Vocal Pattern Families may also have Variants, each with a Distinctive vocalization, as with other Vocal Patterns. They are similarly identified by Roman numeral extensions.

Vocal Pattern Families are listed in the Vocal Pattern Name Column (Column 2), like other Vocal Patterns.

Note 5: Vocal Patterns that are differently spelled but have a similar sound are categorized as different Vocal Patterns. E.g. the end of the words "Sale" and "Pail" are vocalized similarly but as these are spelled differently, they are different Vocal Patterns – each named according to its spelling, (the Vocal Pattern names would correspond with 'AL' and 'AIL' – the Vowel-Consonant Sequences extracted from these examples).

Note 6: In the "Vocal Pattern Vocalization" column (Column 3), a Pause is always only indicated with a dash '-'. This may represent either the Major Pause or the Minor Pause.

In the "Word Example" column (Column 8), Pauses in word examples can be identified as a dash '-' which denotes a Major Pause and a dot '.' which denotes a Minor Pause. However, with Di-Syllabic words – which have one Pause – the dash '-' Symbol is always used to represent the single Pause.

Note 7: In the column, "Vocal Pattern Vocalization" (Column 3), the Vocal Pattern's vocalization is Scripted using the Course's Vocal Fidelity Phonetic System. If a Script Symbol is unfamiliar to you, for clarification, refer as needed to:

> -the Scripting Conventions for Vowel Sounds (Appendix I.B),
> -the Scripting Conventions for Consonant Sounds (Appendix I.C),
> -the Phonetic Symbols for Vowel Sounds (Appendix II.A), and
> -the Phonetic Symbols for Consonant Sounds (Appendix III.C).

Note 8: Often, there are words with relatively small differences in the vocalization of a Vocal Pattern or a Vocal Pattern Variant within them, all of which are acceptable. Where this is so, usually up to two vocalization options are given under the "Vocal Pattern Vocalization" column (Column 2). Options are described using Vocal Fidelity Phonetic Scripting, each separated with a comma. The options include popular and standard vocalizations.

> E.g., the words "Room" and "Shoot" are commonly pronounced with either just an 'O' Long {Ro*o2m, Sho*o2t}, but also frequently with an inserted 'I' Soft preceding the 'O' Long Vowel{R(i)o*o2m, Sh(i)o*o2}. Both articulations are shown, separated by a comma.

The differences in vocalization may be a difference caused by the presence or absence of a Basic Vocal Element, such as:

-an Extension of a Vowel or Consonant Sound,
-an Extension and Repetition of a Vowel Sound,
-the occurrence of the Hiss i.e. '*(h)*' following a particular Consonant,
-the insertion of an External Vowel,
-an audible difference in the Inherent Attributes or Accentuation of a particular Consonant Sound.

It is important to note that the Scripted vocalizations shown do not preclude the existence of other acceptable vocalizations.

Note 9. Certain words have more than one commonly used pronunciation. E.g., the word "Vase" is usually pronounced with an 'A' Hard middle Vowel Sound and the Hissing 'S' (as in "Case", i.e. Consonant Version 'S1'), but it is also sometime pronounced with the 'A' Hard Vowel Sound and the Buzzing 'S' (as in "His", i.e. Version 'S2'). Such word examples with different pronunciations are tagged with the mark '~' in the Word Example column (Column 8). The tag mark indicates that the corresponding Vocal Pattern vocalization is one of more than one commonly used pronunciation of the word example. A tagged word example is also indicative that the word example may be shown again on another row, associated with another Vocal Pattern Variant. In the Table below, the example word "Vase" is tagged ("Vase~") and shown with different pronunciations as a word example under Variants X and XI of the Vocal Pattern 'AS'.

Note 10: In the "LP" or Learning Priority column (Column 4), the Learning Priority of each Vocal Pattern is indicated by a Roman numeral, based on its learning impact on Accent change. Learning Priority has been set to correspond with the Vocal Pattern's Distinctiveness category (APDE) (Column 6).

The most Distinctive Vocal Patterns in the Great Distinctiveness category are Learning Priority I (LP I). Learning these Vocal Patterns delivers great impact on Accent change. LP 'I' Vocal Patterns are covered in the Vocal Pattern Bridge Table in the first Coursebook of the series, "The American Accent Learnway – Cross the Bridge, Over the Divide". Very Distinctive Vocal Patterns in the Substantial Distinctiveness category are LP II. Learning these deliver substantial impact on Accent change. These are covered in the Vocal Pattern Inland Table in the second Coursebook, "The American Accent Learnway – Together, On the Road Inland". Clearly Distinctive Vocal Patterns in the Significant Distinctiveness category are LP III. Learning these deliver significant impact on Accent change. These are covered in the Vocal Pattern Summit Table in the third Coursebook, "The American Accent Learnway – As One, On the Summit".

Note 11: Vocal Patterns are grouped into Learning Sequence (LS) subgroups (Column 5), based on an Estimate of their Rate of Occurrence (RoOE) (Column 7), i.e. upon how often they occur, whether Frequent, Often or Occasional. Within each Learning Priority Group (Note 8 above), those that occur more often are sequenced in the Vocal Pattern Tables before those that occur less often.

In the Vocal Pattern Bridge Table, within Priority Group 'I', Vocal Patterns in LS subgroup 1 are those that Occur Frequently and are presented first. Vocal Patterns in LS subgroup 2 are those that Occur Often and are presented next. Vocal Patterns in LS subgroup 3 are those that Occur Occasionally and are presented last. Similarly, in the Vocal Pattern Inland Table, within Priority Group 'II', Vocal Patterns in LS subgroup 4 are those that Occur Frequently and are presented first. Vocal Patterns in LS subgroup 5 are those that Occur Often and are presented next. Vocal Patterns in LS subgroup 6 are those that Occur Occasionally and are presented last. And again, similarly, in the Vocal Pattern Summit Table, within Priority Group 'III', Vocal Patterns in LS subgroup 7 are those that Occur Frequently and are presented first. Vocal Patterns in LS subgroup 8 are those that Often Occur Often and are presented next. Vocal Patterns in LS subgroup 9 are those that Occur Occasionally and are presented last.

Note 12: In the column "APDE" (Column 6), the American Pronunciation Distinctiveness Estimate is shown for each Vocal Pattern.

In the Vocal Pattern Bridge Table, the Vocal Patterns are all graded 'A', i.e. in the Great Distinctiveness category, indicating that they are the most Distinctive Vocal Patterns. In the Vocal Pattern Inland Table, they are all graded 'B', i.e. in the Substantial Distinctiveness category, indicating that they are very Distinctive Vocal Patterns. In the Vocal Pattern Summit Table, they are all graded 'C', i.e. in the Significant Distinctiveness category, indicating that they are clearly Distinctive Vocal Patterns.

Note 13: In the "RoOE" column (Column 7), the Rate of Occurrence Estimate shows how often a Vocal Pattern is estimated to Occur in the Language. Rates of Occurrence may be Frequent (Fre), Often (Oft) or Occasional (Occ).

Note 14. Each Vocal Pattern in the Vocal Pattern Table below may be referenced to a corresponding Word List Table (in a separate Chapter, per the Table of Contents), when there are enough additional word examples containing the Vocal Pattern to require a separate Table. The Word Lists for each Vocal Pattern further enable you to convert your pronunciation of a larger number of words at one time, rather than only one word at a time. Word List Tables are not provided for Vocal Patterns that have an Occasional Rate of Occurrence.

Word List Tables can be looked up from information provided with each Vocal Pattern, in the Table below. If a Word List Table has been provided, the "Word List Table Y/N" column (Column 10) will show 'Y', to indicate that, "Yes", a corresponding Word List Table has been provided and may be looked up from referral information on that row. (If no Word List Table has been provided, then the column will show 'N', meaning that, "No", do not look for a corresponding Word List Table as there isn't one).

Word List Tables are presented in the same order as in the Vocal Pattern Tables. If a Word List Table for a Vocal Pattern has been provided (as indicated in Column 10), it will be in order of its Learning Priority Number (Column 4), its Learning Sequence Number (Column 5) and according to the alphanumeric order of its name – including the Roman Numeral Extension in the name, if any (Column 2).

The first row of each Word List Table shows the Vocal Pattern Priority-Sequence category, which is the Vocal Pattern's Learning Priority number (from Column 4 of the Vocal Pattern Table below) and its Learning Sequence number (from Column 5 of the Vocal Pattern Table below), separated by an oblique, e.g. 'I/3' or 'II/4'. The second row of each Word List Table shows the Vocal Pattern Name (from Column 2) of the Vocal Pattern Table below. Word Lists are grouped within each Priority-Sequence category in alphanumeric order of the Vocal Pattern name.

Accordingly, Vocal Pattern Variants 'AN' - I' and 'AN - II, being in the same Priority-Sequence category 'I/1', have Word List Tables following each other consecutively, as in the Vocal Pattern Table. By contrast, though 'IN - I' (Priority-Sequence: I/1) and 'IN - II' (Priority-Sequence:'II/5') follow each other alphanumerically, the corresponding Word List Tables do not follow each other consecutively as they are in separate Priority-Sequence categories. 'IN - I' follows 'IM - I' and 'IN - II' follows 'IM - II' in alphanumeric order in their respective Priority-Sequence categories in different Vocal Pattern Tables.

Note 15. In the second last Column, "Change OK/C", you can identify the Vocal Patterns you do not articulate in the American way. Mark those that you already articulate as do Americans 'OK', for "No Change Needed" and those that you don't as 'C' for "Change Needed". By assessing yourself on each Vocal Pattern in the Table, you will create a custom learning list based on your specific way of speaking, targeting the specific Vocal Patterns that you need to change. You will identify exactly how many and which Vocal Patterns you need to relearn. You can then proceed to change blocks of words that correspond with each Vocal Pattern at one time. A good indication that change for a particular Vocal Pattern is needed is if you find that you vocalize the Vocal Pattern in one or more of the example words in different ways.

Note 16. Distinctive Vocal Patterns in the Great, Substantial or Significant, Distinctiveness categories can be looked up in the Vocal Pattern Tables. The most Distinctive Vocal Patterns are listed in the Vocal Pattern Bridge Table. Very Distinctive Vocal Patterns are listed in the Vocal Pattern Inland Table. Clearly Distinctive Vocal Patterns are listed in the Vocal Pattern Summit Table. The Bridge Table is provided in Coursebook One, "The American Accent Learnway – Cross the Bridge, Over the Divide" of this three Coursebook series. The Inland Table is provided in Coursebook Two, "The American Accent Learnway – Together, On the Road Inland". The Summit Table is provided in Coursebook Three, "The American Accent Learnway – As One, On the Summit".

If a particular Vocal Pattern is not listed, it is most likely of Insignificant Distinctiveness, meaning that the Vocal Pattern was not sufficiently different to include in the Bridge, Inland or Summit Tables.

Vocal Patterns of Insignificant Distinctiveness are only included in the Master Table and not otherwise listed, as there is too small or no difference between how these are vocalized in the American Accent and British Accent.

If you encounter a word that has an unusual articulation of a Vocal Pattern that does not match any of the Variants in any of the Vocal Pattern Tables, i.e. the Vocal Pattern Bridge, Inland or Summit Tables, it could be that it is an Irregular Vowel-Consonant Sequence. A Table: "Vocalizing Words With Irregular Vowel Consonant Sequences" is included as Appendix IV.

You may sometimes find that a specific Vocal Pattern has been left out of the Vocal Pattern Tables provided in the Coursebooks. This could be because Vocal Patterns that are not Distinctive are only listed in the Vocal Pattern Master Table. Also, it is simply not possible to ensure inclusion of each and every Vocal Pattern.

Copyright © published 2022 by Adil Rehman.

							Columns		
1	2	3	4	5	6	7	8	9	10
Serial	Vocal Pattern Name	Vocal Pattern Vocalization	LP	LS	APDE	RoOE	Word Example with Vocal Pattern (Pauses shown)	Change OK/ C	Word List Table Y/N
1	AT - I	a"*T(h)*, a*T(h)*	II	4	B	Fre	At, Bat, Brat, Cat, Flat, Gnat, Hat, Mat, Pat, Rat, Sat, Spat, That.		N
2	ER - IV	e-*r*	II	4	B	Fre	Aus-te-ri.ty, Cle-ric~, E-rro-neous~, Me-rit~, Me-rry, Pe-ril~, Ve-ry.		Y

3	ICK - I	ic*K(h), i"c*K(h)	II	4	B	Fre	Click, Flick, Pick, Sick, Slick, Trick.		Y
4	IL - II	i"L'l*, i'L'l	II	4	B	Fre	Bill, Drill, Fills, Frills, Hill, Mill, Pill, Till, Skilled, Still, Will.		Y
5	ING - I	i[ng]1, i'[ng]1	II	4	B	Fre	Bring, Fling, Ring, Swing, Sting, Wing.		Y
6	IS - I	i"S1, i'S1	II	4	B	Fre	Chris, This, Kiss, Hiss, Miss.		N
7	ITH - I	i"[TH], i[TH]	II	4	B	Fre	Kith, Pith, Smith, With.		N
8	OF - I	o'F, oF	II	4	B	Fre	Off, Scoff.		N
9	ON - II	o'N	II	4	B	Fre	Con, Gone~, Jon, On~, Ron.		N
10	OO^ - I	o2o*^, (i)o2o*^	II	4	B	Fre	Boots, Food, Moon, Mood, Noon, Rooms, Soon, Scoot, Shoot.		Y
11	OT - I	o'T(h)	II	4	B	Fre	Cot, Dot, Got, Hot, Jot, Lot, Not, Pot, Plot, Rot, Slot, Trot.		Y
12	OT - II	o'-t2*([td]), o'-t	II	4	B	Fre	O-tter, Blo-tter, Co-tter, Clo-tted, Go-tten, Ho-tter, Ro-tter, Slo-tted.		Y
13	OUR - II	o*(a)-(W)u1R, o*(a)-u1R	II	4	B	Fre	Ho-ur~, Flo-ur, Lo-ur, O-ur~, Sco-ur, So-ur.		N
14	OUR - III	o*(a)-(w)u1R	II	4	B	Fre	Hou-rs, Lou-red, Ou-rs, Scou-red. Sou-red.		N

15	OW - I	o*(a)'w	II	4	B	Fre	Brown, Cow, Crowd, How, Flow-er, Now, Owl, Prow-ess, Tow-er.		Y
16	AB - I	a'B, a''B	II	5	B	Oft	Crab, Drab, Flab, Jab, Lab, Nab, Slab, Tab.		Y
17	AB - II	a'B, a''B	II	5	B	Oft	Abbs, Cabbed, Crabs, Jabbed, Nabbed, Slabs.		Y
18	ADG	a''-d*g*(j), a-d*g*(j)	II	5	B	Oft	Ba-dger, Ga-dget.		N
19	AG - I	a'G1(h)	II	5	B	Oft	Bag, Flag, Lag, Stag, Tag, Wag.		Y
20	AG - II	a'G1	II	5	B	Oft	Bagged, Flags, Lagged, Mag-net, Rags, Sagged, Tagged.		Y
21	AG - III	a'-g1, a-g1	II	5	B	Oft	Ba-ggage, Bra-gging, Dra-gon, Ma-ggot, Ra-gged, Wa-gon.		Y
22	AIR - I	a*i*(e)'R'	II	5	B	Oft	Blair, Chair, Fair, Flair, Hair, Lair, Pair, Stair.		Y
23	AIR - II	a*i*(e)'R', a*i*(e)'R	II	5	B	Oft	Chaired, Chairs, Paired, Pairs, Flairs, Stairs.		Y
24	AL - I	a*(o)'L'	II	5	B	Oft	Al-ter, Bald, Bal-tic, Call, Called, Falls, Hal-ter, Malt, Sal-ted.		Y
25	AL - II	a*(o)-l	II	5	B	Oft	A-ppa-lling, Ca-llers, Fa-lling, Sta-lling, Swa-llow, Wa-llow.		Y
26	AM - II	a''-m, a'-m	II	5	B	Oft	A-ma-teur, Ca-la-mi.ty, Ca-me-ra, Sta-mi.na, Sla-mming. Tra-mmel.		Y

27	AM - III	a"M, a'M	II	5	B	Oft	Amplify, Camped, Lamp, Rammed, Ram, Sam, Stamp, Trample.		Y
28	AN - III	a"N, a'N	II	5	B	Oft	An-ge-la, At-lan-tic, Can-dor, Fran-tic, Stan-dard, Tan-gent.		Y
29	AN - IV	a'-N, a-N	II	5	B	Oft	A-nna, Ca-na-da, Ca-ni.ster, Gra-nite, Ma-nners, Pla-net, Sa-nity.		Y
30	ANC - I	a"nc*($S1$), a'nc*($S1$)	II	5	B	Oft	Chance, Dance, Fi-nance, France, Ro-mance, Stance, Trance.		Y
31	ANC - II	a"nc*($S1$), a'nc*($S1$)	II	5	B	Oft	Chanced, Danced, En-hanced, Fi-nanced, Pranced.		N
32	ANC - III	a"N-c*($s1$), a'N-c*($s1$)	II	5	B	Oft	Can-cel, Chan-cy, Dan-cer, Dan-cing, Fan-cy, Nan-cy, Pran-cing.		Y
33	AND - II	a"N-D, a'N-D	II	5	B	Oft	A-ban-don, Bran-ding, Can-did, Man-da-tory, Ran-dom, San-dal.		Y
34	ANG - I	a'[ng1]-($g1$)	II	5	B	Oft	Ang-er, Ang-us, Bang-les, Dang-le, Mang-o, Tang-led, Wrang-ler.		Y
35	ANG - II	a'[ng1]	II	5	B	Oft	Bang, Clang, Fang, Hangs, Ha-rangue, Rang, Sang, Slang.		Y
36	ANS - II	a"N-$s1$, a'N-$s1$	II	5	B	Oft	An-swer, Ex-pan-sive, Tran-si-tive.		N
37	ANS - III	a"nS1, anS1	II	5	B	Oft	Trans-fer, Trans-form, Trans-pon-der, Trans-port, Trans-por-ta-tion.		N
38	ANT - IV	aN-T, a"N-T	II	5	B	Oft	Gran-ted, Fran-tic, Pan-ting, Pan-try, Se-man-tic, Shan-ty.		Y

39	AP - II	a' P	II	5	B	Oft	A-dapt, A-dap-ta-tion~, E-lapse, Flaps, Maps, Rapt, Trapped.		Y
40	AP - III	a'-P, a''-P	II	5	B	Oft	A-ppa-ra.tus, A-ppe.tite, Ca-pi-tal, Ha-ppen, Ra-pid, Ta-ppet.		Y
41	AR - V	a*(e)-r	II	5	B	Oft	A-qua.ri.um, Ca-rry, Ja.nu-a.ry, Li-bra.ry, Ma-ry, Va-ri.ous.		Y
42	AR - VI	a*(o)R	II	5	B	Oft	Quark, Quartz, Quar-ter, Qua-rrel, War, Ward, War-den, Warp.		N
43	AS - IV	a'-s1	II	5	B	Oft	A-si-nine, A-scer-tain, Cla-ssi-cal, Fa.sci-nate, Ha-ssle, Pa-ssive.		Y
44	AST - II	a'S1-t	II	5	B	Oft	As-te-risk, As-ton, As-tro-naut, Fas-ti-dious, Pas-tel, Cas-ta-way.		Y
45	AT - II	a''T, aT	II	5	B	Oft	Bats, Cats, Mats, Hats, Pats, Rats, Slats, Stats, Vats.		N
46	AT - III	a-t2*([td])t*, a-tt*	II	5	B	Oft	Ba-ttle, Ba-tte-ry, Ca-ttle, Ma-tter, Ra-ttle, Se-attle, Sha-tter.		Y
47	AT - IV	A-t2*([td]), A-t	II	5	B	Oft	Ca-ter, Cra-ter, De-fla-ted, In-fla-ted, La-ter, Ra-ted, Po-ta-to.		Y
48	ATCH - I	a''t*[CH](h), at*[CH](h)	II	5	B	Oft	Batch, Catch, Dis-patch, Latch, Match, Patch, Snatch, Thatch.		N
49	AU^ - I	a*u*(o)'-^, a*u*(o)(w)-^	II	5	B	Oft	Au-dio, Au-to, Au-thor, Dau-ghter, Rau-cous.		Y
50	AU^ - II	a*(o)'u*^ a*(o)u*(w)^	II	5	B	Oft	Caught, Caulk, Fraud, Laud, Haul, Pause, Sauce, Taunt, Taut.		Y

51	AU^ - III	a*(o)'u*-^ a*(o)u*(w)-^	II	5	B	Oft	Cau-tion, Dau-ghter, Hau-ling, Lau-ding, Nau-sea, Pau-sing.		Y
52	AUGH - I	a*(o)'u*[gh]* a*(o)u*(w) [gh]*	II	5	B	Oft	Caught, Dis-traught, Fraught, Naught, Taught.		N
53	AUGH - II	au*[gh]*(F)	II	5	B	Oft	Draught~, Draugh-ting, Draughts~, Laughs, Laughed, Laugh-ter.		N
54	AUGH - III	a*(o)'u*[gh]*-^, a*(o)u*(w) [gh]*-^	II	5	B	Oft	Daugh-ter, Haugh-ty, Naugh-ty.		N
55	AW	a*(o)w	II	5	B	Oft	Awe, Aw-ful, Bawl, Flaw, Hawk, Law-yer, Saw, Traw-ler.		Y
56	EATH - I	e"a*[TH], ea1[TH]	II	5	B	Oft	Breath, Death-ly.		N
57	EC - I	e'C(h), eC(h)	II	5	B	Oft	Check, Deck, Fleck, Neck, Peck, Wreck.		N
58	ED - II	e'D, e"D	II	5	B	Oft	Beds, Fred's, Keds, Reds, Sleds, Sheds, Sped, Ted's, Weds.		N
59	ED - III	E'D, ED	II	5	B	Oft	Bu-rried, Cu-rried, Ma-rried, Hu-rried, Scu-rried, Wo-rried.		Y
60	EDG - I	e"d*g*(J)(h), e'd*g*(J)(h)	II	5	B	Oft	Dredge, Hedge, Ledge, Pledge, Sedge, Sledge, Wedge.		N
61	EF - II	e F, e"F	II	5	B	Oft	Be-reft, Cleft, Deft, Heft, Left, Theft.		N
62	EG - I	e"G(h), e G(h)	II	5	B	Oft	Beg, Egg, Keg, Leg, Meg, Peg.		N

63	EN - III	e"N, e'N	II	5	B	Oft	A-men-ded, Ex-ten-ded, In-ten-ded, Ren-ted, Un-a-tten-ded.		Y
64	EN - IV	e*n*, e-*n*	II	5	B	Oft	Cen-ter/Ce-nter, En-ter/E-nter, Ren-ter/Re-nter.		Y
65	ENCH - I	e"n[*CH*](*h*), en[*CH*](*h*)	II	5	B	Oft	Bench, Drenched, French, Hench-men, Stench, Wrenched.		N
66	END - I	e'*n*D(*h*), e"*n*D(*h*)	II	5	B	Oft	A-scend, A-mend, De-fend, Fend, In-tend, Pre-tend.		Y
67	ENT - I	e'*n*T(*h*), e"*n*T(*h*)	II	5	B	Oft	A-scent, Bent, In-tent, Re-sent, Pre-sent, Pre-vent, Re-lent.		Y
68	ENT - II	e*n*-t2*([td]), e-*nt**	II	5	B	Oft	Cen-ter/Ce-nter, Den-ted/De-nted, En-ter/E-nter, Ren-tal/Re-ntal.		Y
69	ER - V	e1R	II	5	B	Oft	Cer-ti.fy, Co-mmer-cial, Di-verge, Er-mine, Mer-ges, Ver-ti-cal.		Y
70	ERN - I	e1RN	II	5	B	Oft	Eas-tern, Fern, Lec-tern, Nor-thern, Sou-thern, Wes-tern.		Y
71	ERN - II	e1R'-*n*	II	5	B	Oft	Er-nest, In-ter-nal, Mo.der-ni-za-tion, Wes-ter-ni-za-tion.		Y
72	ESH - I	e"[*SH*], e'[*SH*]	II	5	B	Oft	Flesh, Fresh, Mesh, Thresh.		N
73	ET - II	e-t2*([td]), e-*t*	II	5	B	Oft	Be-tter, Ke-ttle, Fre-tting, Me-tal,Se-tter, Se-ttle.		Y
74	ET - III	E'-t2*([td]), E'-*t*	II	5	B	Oft	Com-pe-ting, Gree-ter, Gree-ting, Pe-ter, Me-ter, Tee-ter.		Y

75	ETCH - I	e"t*[CH](h), et*[CH](h)	II	5	B	Oft	Fetch, Fetched, Ketch, Retch, Sketch, Sketched, Wretch.		N
76	ETT	e-t2*([td])t*	II	5	B	Oft	Be-tter, Fe-tters, Ge-tting, Ke-ttle, Le-tter, Pe-tted, Se-tter.		Y
77	EW^ - I	e*(i)(u2)w^, e*(u2)'w^	II	5	B	Oft	Crew, Flew, Lewd, News, Stew.		Y
78	EW^ - II	e*(i)(u2)-w, e*(u2)'-w	II	5	B	Oft	Bre-wing, Cre-wing, Che-wing, Re-ne-wal~, Ste-wing~.		Y
79	IB - I	i"B,	II	5	B	Oft	Bib, Crib, Fib, Jib, Nib, Rib.		N
80	IBUT - I	i-bUT, i-BUT	II	5	B	Oft	A-ttri.butes, Con-tri.butes, Dis-tri.butes, Tri-butes.		N
81	IBUT - II	i-bU-t*(d)	II	5	B	Oft	Con-tri-bu.ted, Con-tri.bu-tor, Dis.tri.bu-ting, Dis-tri.bu-tor.		Y
82	IE^ - I	i*E'^	II	5	B	Oft	Be-lief, Bu-llied, Ca-rried, Fiend, Frieze, Grief, Lien, Hu-rried.		Y
83	IG - I	iG, i'G	II	5	B	Oft	Big, Brig, Fig, Gig, Jig, Rig, Wig.		N
84	IGHT - I	I'g*h*-t2*([td]), I'g*h*-t	II	5	B	Oft	Brigh-ten, En-ligh-ten, Figh-ting, Migh-ty, Sigh-ting, Tigh-ten.		Y
85	IL - III	I'L', I(a1)L'	II	5	B	Oft	Bile, De-file, File, Mile, Re-vile, Smile.		Y
86	IM - II	I'M, (a2)IM	II	5	B	Oft	Chime, Climbed, Dimes, Grime, Lime, Prime, Slime, Time.		Y

87	IN – II	I'N, (a2)IN	II	5	B	Oft	Bind, Blinds, Di-vine, Fine, Line, Grind, Kind, Mind, Pint.		Y
88	INCH - I	i"n[CH](h), i'n[CH](h)	II	5	B	Oft	Inch, Cinch, Cinched, Clinch, Clinched, Flinched, Winched.		N
89	IND - I	i"nD(h), i'nD(h)	II	5	B	Oft	Wind~, Re-scind.		N
90	ING - II	i'[ng]2*(J)(h), i"[ng]2*(J)(h)	II	5	B	Oft	Binge, Cringe, Fringe, In-fringe, Singe, Syringe, Tinge, Whinge.		N
91	ING - III	i'[ng]2*(J), i"[ng]2*(J)	II	5	B	Oft	Binged, Cringed, Fringed, Singed, Tinged, Whinged.		N
92	INS - I	i"ns*(Z), ins*(Z)	II	5	B	Oft	Bins, Fins, Grins, Pins, Shins, Spins, Tins, Wins.		N
93	INT - II	i"nT	II	5	B	Oft	Mints, Stints, Prints, Tints.		N
94	INT - III	iN-t2*([td]), iN-t, iN-T	II	5	B	Oft	Min-ted, Min-ting, Prin-ting, Prin-ted, Sprin-ted, Sprin-ting, Tin-ted.		N
95	IR - I	I(a1)R', I'R'	II	5	B	Oft	Fire, Ire, De-si.re, In-spire, Mire, Re-tire, Tire, Wire.		Y
96	IR - II	I(a1)R, I'R	II	5	B	Oft	Fires, Desires, Desired, Inspired, Mired, Tired, Spires.		Y
97	IR - III	i1R	II	5	B	Oft	Bird, Cir-cle, Fir, Sir, Sir-loin, Squirm, Squirt.		Y
98	IS - II	i"S1, i'S1	II	5	B	Oft	Brisk, Disc, E-xist, Gist, Grist, Lists, Mist, Re-sist, Whisk, Wrist.		Y

99	ISH - I	i"[SH], i[SH]	II	5	B	Oft	Dish, Fish, Wish.		N
100	ITCH - I	i"t*[CH](h), i"t*[CH](h)	II	5	B	Oft	Ditch, Ditched, Hitch, Itch, Itched, Glitch, Snitch, Stitch, Witch.		N
101	IV - I	i"V, iV	II	5	B	Oft	Give, Gives, Live~, Lives~.		N
102	OC - I	o'C(h)	II	5	B	Oft	Block, Clock, Flock, Knock, Lock, Rock, Shock, Stock.		Y
103	OC - II	o'C	II	5	B	Oft	Doc-tor, Mocked, Oc-ta-gon, Oc-to-ber, Oc-to-pus, Rocks.		Y
104	OC - III	o'-c, o'-C	II	5	B	Oft	Blo-cking, Cro-co-dile, Mo-cca-ssin, Ro-cker, So-ccer.		Y
105	OD - I	o'D(h)	II	5	B	Oft	Clod, Cod, God, Nod, Plod, Pod, Rod, Sod, Shod, Tod, Trod.		N
106	OD - II	o'D	II	5	B	Oft	Clods, Nods, Plods, Pods, Rods.		N
107	OD - III	o'-D	II	5	B	Oft	Bo-dy, Co-di-fi-ca-tion, Mo-del, Mo-dern, Mo-di-fy, Sho-ddy.		Y
108	ODG - I	o'-[dg]*(J)	II	5	B	Oft	Co-dger, Lo-dging, Lo-dges, Ro-dger, Sto-dgy.		N
109	OF - II	o'F, oF, o)'F	II	5	B	Oft	A-loft, Of-ten, Loft, Lof-ty, Sof-ten.		N
110	OF - III	o'-f	II	5	B	Oft	Co-ffer, O-ffense~, O-ffer, O-ffe-ring, O-ffi-cer, Pro-ffer, To-ffee.		N

111	OG - I	o'*G*	II	5	B	Oft	A-na-logue, Blog, Ca-ta-logue, Dog, Flog, Hog, Log, Slog.		Y
112	OG - II	o'G	II	5	B	Oft	Blogs, Cogs, Flogged, Frogs, Logs, Slogged, Slogs.		Y
113	OG - III	o'-G, o'-*g*	II	5	B	Oft	Lo-gger, Lo-gging, O-ggle, Slo-gger, To-ggle.		Y
114	OG - IV	o'-g2*(*j*)	II	5	B	Oft	Co-gi-tate, Ho-mo-ge.nize, Lo-gic, Lo-gical, Pe-da-go-gi.cal.		Y
115	OL - I	o)'L', o'L'	II	5	B	Oft	A-toll, Col, Di-ssolve, Dolls~, Re-solve, Solve~, Sol-vent~.		N
116	OL - II	o'-l, o'-*l*	II	5	B	Oft	Co-llege, Fo-llow, Ho-li-day, Mo-le-cule, Po-llen, Po-li-tics, So-lid.		Y
117	OM - II	o'-*m*	II	5	B	Oft	Co-met, Co-mmerce, Do-mi-nant, No-mi-nate, To-mmy.		Y
118	ON - III	o)'*N*', o*N*'	II	5	B	Oft	Gone~, On~, Ne-on, Salon, Shone.		Y
119	ON - IV	o'N	II	5	B	Oft	Ab-scond, Con-tact, Con-tour, Con-sole, Fronds, Mon-ster.		Y
120	ON - V	o'-*n*	II	5	B	Oft	A-no-ny-mous, Ho-no-ra.ble, I-co-nic, Ho-nest, So-nic.		Y
121	ONG - I	o)'[ng], o[ng]	II	5	B	Oft	A-long, Be-long, Long, Prong, Song, Strong, Throng, Tong.		Y
122	OO^ - II	O2o*-^, (i)o2o*-^	II	5	B	Oft	Bloo-ming, Gloo-my, Moo-dy, Roo-ted, Schoo-ner, Soo-ner.		Y

123	OP - I	o'P(h)	II	5	B	Oft	Cop, Crop, Hop, Flop, Pop, Prop, Shop, Sop, Stop, Top.		Y
124	OP - II	o'P	II	5	B	Oft	Drops, Flops, Hopped, Mopped, Shops, Shops, Stopped.		Y
125	OP - III	o'-P	II	5	B	Oft	Ho-pping, Mi.cro-sco.pic, O-pe-rate, Pro-per, Tro-pic, Tro-pical.		Y
126	ORR - I	o)'-*rr**, o-*rr**	II	5	B	Oft	Co.rres-pon-dent, Ho.rri-ble, Lo.rry, Po-rridge, To-rrid.		Y
127	ORR - II	o'-*rr**	II	5	B	Oft	Bo-rrow~, So-rrow~, So-rry~, To-morrow~.		N
128	OS - I	o'S1	II	5	B	Oft	Hos.pi.tal, Cos-by, Cos-tume, Moss, Os-trich, Pos-thu.mous~.		Y
129	OS - II	o'-*s*1s*	II	5	B	Oft	Cro-ssing, Flo-ssing, Po-ssi.ble, To-ssing, Lo-sses, Mo-ssy.		Y
130	OSH - I	o'[SH]	II	5	B	Oft	Gosh, Josh, Posh, Slosh.		N
131	OST - I	o'S1	II	5	B	Oft	Cost, Frost, Lost, Post-hu.mous~.		N
132	OTCH - I	o't*[CH](h)	II	5	B	Oft	Botch, Botched, Blotch, Notch, Scotch, Splotch.		N
133	OTH - II	o1.[t(d)h]	II	5	B	Oft	A-no-ther, Bro-thers, O-ther, Mo-ther. Smo-thered.		N
134	OU^ - II	ou*^	II	5	B	Oft	Bought, Cough, Sought, Thought, Wrought, You'll.		N

135	OU^ - III	o*(a)-(w)u1^ o*(a)-u1^	II	5	B	Oft	Do-ur, Fo-ul, Ho-ur~, Lo-ur, O-ur~, So-ur, Sco-ur.		N
136	OUGH T	o)'[gh]*T(h), o[gh]*T(h)	II	5	B	Oft	Bought, Fought, Ought, Sought, Thought, Wrought.		N
137	OUR - IV	o)'u*R, ou*R	II	5	B	Oft	Poured, Pours, Your's.		N
138	OUR - V	o1'u*R	II	5	B	Oft	A-djourn, Jour-nal, Jour-na-list, Jour-ney.		N
139	UA^ - I	u*(W)a*(o)^	II	5	B	Oft	Gua-va, E-qua-li.ty, Quan-ti.ty, Squa-tter, Squall, Squan-der.		Y
140	UAR - II	U-a*(e)-r	II	5	B	Oft	Es-tu-a.ry, Ja.nu-a.ry, Feb-ru-a.ry, Sanc.tu-a.ry.		N
141	UN - I	u1N	II	5	B	Oft	Bun, Dun, Fun, Pun, Run, Stun, Stun.		N
142	UN - II	u1N	II	5	B	Oft	A-sun-der, Bun-ting, Grun-ted, Un-der, Hun-ter, Sun-day, Shun-ted.		Y
143	UR - II	u1R', u1R	II	5	B	Oft	A-zure, Burr, Cen-sure, Lec-ture, O-ccur, Sure, Spur.		Y
144	UR - III	u1R	II	5	B	Oft	Burn, Curl, Cur-tain, Turn, Surge, Spurt, Sur-pass, Un-furl.		Y
145	UR - IV	u(o)R', uR'	II	5	B	Oft	Ab-jure, A-ssure, En-sure, I-nure~, Lure, Sure~.		N
146	UR - V	u1-r	II	5	B	Oft	Bu-ry, Can-ter-bu.ry, Cen-tu.ry, Cu-rry, Cu-rrent, Flu-rry, Hu-rry.		Y

147	URN - I	u1R'*N*	II	5	B	Oft	Ad-journ, Burn, Churn, Spurn, Turn, Urn.		N
148	US - I	u2-s3*([*zh*])	II	5	B	Oft	Con-clu-sion, De-lu-sion, I-llu-sion, Ex-clu-sion, In-clu-sion.		Y
149	UT - I	U-t2*([td]), U-t	II	5	B	Oft	Com-pu-ter, Dis-tri.bu-ting, E-lec-tro-cu-ted, E-xe-cu-tor, Re-fu-ting.		Y
150	UT - II	u1-t2*([td])t*	II	5	B	Oft	Bu-tter, Cu-tting, Flu-tter, Mu-tter, Re-bu-ttal, Shu-tting Stu-tter.		Y
151	UT - III	u2-t2*([td]), u2-t	II	5	B	Oft	Du-ty, Flu-ted, Sa-lu-ted, Sa-lu-ting~.		N
152	UTT	u1-t2*([td]), u1-t	II	5	B	Oft	Bu-tter, Cu-tting, Clu-tter, Flu-tter, Mu-tter, Pu-tted, Shu-tter.		Y
153	AG - IV	a2g3*([*ZH*])	II	6	B	Occ	Co-llage, Ga-rage, Ma-ssage.		N
154	AG - V	a2-g3*([*zh*])'	II	6	B	Occ	Co-lla-ges, Ga-ra-ges, Ma-ssa-ge.		N
155	ALT - I	a*(o)L*T(h)*	II	6	B	Occ	Ba-salt, E-xalt, Halt, Malt, Salt, Walt, Waltz.		N
156	ALT - II	a*(o)L'-*t*	II	6	B	Occ	Al-ter-nate, Dal-ton, Wal-ter, Fal-[ter], Mal-ta.		N
157	ANCH - I	a"n[*CH*]*(h)*	II	6	B	Occ	Blanch, Branch.		N
158	ANG - III	a"N-g2*(j)*	II	6	B	Occ	An-ge-la, Los An-ge-les, Tan-ge-rine, Tan-gent, Tan-gen.tial.		N

159	ANS - IV	aN-s2*(z)	II	6	B	Occ	Tran-si-tion, Tran-si-to-ry, Trans-for-ming, Trans-for-mer.		N
160	AR - VII	a1R	II	6	B	Occ	A-nar-chist~, Le-thar-gy, Mo-nar-chist~, Mo-nar-chy~.		N
161	ARCH - VII	a1R-[ch]*k	II	6	B	Occ	A-nar-chist~, A-nar-chy~, Mo-nar-chist~, Mo-nar-chy~.		N
162	AS - V	a'-s*(sh)s*, a"-s*(sh)s*	II	6	B	Occ	Com-pa-ssion, Com-pa-ssio.nate, Pa-ssion, Pa-ssio.nate,		N
163	ASM - I	a'-s2*(Z)M	II	6	B	Occ	Cha-sm, En-thu-sia.sm, I-co-no-cla.sm, Spas-m.		N
164	ASS - II	a'-s1s*	II	6	B	Occ	A-sset, Cla-ssi-cal, Ma-ssive, Pa-ssive.		N
165	ASS - III	a'-s*(sh)s*, a"-s*(sh)s*	II	6	B	Occ	Com-pa-ssion, Com-pa-ssio.nate, Pa-ssion, Pa-ssio.nate.		N
166	AV - I	a'-v, a"-v	II	6	B	Occ	Ca-ve.at~, Ca-val-ry, Ga-vel, Ja-ve-lin, Tra-vel, Tra-ve-lling,		N
167	AX - I	a"x*(K)(S1'), a'x*(K)(S1').	II	6	B	Occ	Re-lax, Re-laxed, Flax, Max, Pax, Tax, Taxed, Wax, Waxed.		N
168	ENG - I	e"nG(h)	II	6	B	Occ	A-venge, Re-venge, Venge-ful.		N
169	EON - I	E-oN, E-o'N	II	6	B	Occ	E-on, Fre-on, Le-on, Ne-on, Pe-on.		N
170	ERR - I	e'-rr*	II	6	B	Occ	Bur-be.rry, Blue-be.rry, Cran-be.rry, E-rrand, Me-rry, Te-rri-tory.		N

171	ETH - I	e"[TH]	II	6	B	Occ	Beth, Seth.		N
172	IA^ - I	I-a1^	II	6	B	Occ	Di.al, Li.ar, Fri.ar, Tri.al, Vi.al.		N
173	IA^ - II	i*(E)-a^	II	6	B	Occ	Co-ri-an-der, Fi..as-co, I-li.ad, Li.ana~, Ti.ara.		N
174	IAR - II	I'a1R	II	6	B	Occ	Bri-ar, Fi-ar, Li-ar.		N
175	IE^ - II	i*E(e1)^	II	6	B	Occ	A-lien, Bier, Field, Mien, Pier, Shield, Wield.		N
176	INX	i"[nx]*([nKS]), i[nx]*([nKS])	II	6	B	Occ	Jinx, Minx.		N
177	IO^ - I	I-o'^	II	6	B	Occ	An-ti-bi.o-tics, Bi.o-lo-gy, Bi.o-nic, I-on~.		N
178	IO^ - III	i*(E)-o'	II	6	B	Occ	A-vi.o-nics, Cu-ri.o-si.ty, His-tri.o-nics.		N
179	OD G - II	o'[dg]*(J)(h)	II	6	B	Occ	Dodge, Dodged, Lodged.		N
180	OLL - II	o)'L'1*, o'L'1*	II	6	B	Occ	A-toll~, Doll~, Dolls~, Dolled~, Moll~.		N
181	ONG - II	o)'[ng]-(g), o[ng]-(g)	II	6	B	Occ	Be-long-ing, Long-ing, Long-ish, Strong-er.		N
182	ONK - I	o'[nK](h), o)'[nK](h)	II	6	B	Occ	Bonk, Clonk, Honk.		N

183	OOR - I	oo*R	II	6	B	Occ	Door, Floor, Floored, Moor~, Poor~.		N
184	OOR - II	o*(u)o, o*o*(u)	II	6	B	Occ	Moor~, Poor~.		N
185	OOR - III	oo*-r	II	6	B	Occ	Floo-ring, Moo-rish, Moo-ring.		N
186	OPH - II	o'-p*h*(f)	II	6	B	Occ	Ca-ta-stro.phic, So-phi-stry, So-phism.		N
187	OS - III	o'-s2	II	6	B	Occ	Clo-set, De-po-site, Po-si-tive, Re-po.si-to.ry.		N
188	OSH - II	o'-[sh]	II	6	B	Occ	Slo-shing.		N
189	OST - II	o'S1-t	II	6	B	Occ	Fos-ter, Hos-tel, Im-pos-ter, Os-trich, Ros-ter.		N
190	OTCH - II	o'-t*[ch]	II	6	B	Occ	Blo-tches, Blo-tching, Cro-che.ty.		N
191	OTH - III	o'-[th]	II	6	B	Occ	Fro-thing, Fro-thy, Go-tham, Go-thic.		N
192	OX - I	o'x*(K)(S1)	II	6	B	Oft	Box, Cox, Fox, Ox, Pox.		N
193	OX - II	o'x*(K)-(s1)	II	6	B	Occ	Bo-xer, No-xious, Pa-ro.xysm, Ob-no.xious, O.xy-mo-ron, To-xin.		N
194	UA^ - II	u2-a2^	II	6	B	Occ	E-du.ar-do~, Nu-ance~.		N

195	UI^ - III	U-i^	II	6	B	Occ	I-nnu.it, In-ge-nu-i.ty~, Tu.i-tion~.		N
196	UN - III	u2'N, (i)u2N	II	6	B	Occ	Dune~, June, Tune~.		N
197	UN - IV	u2'N, (i)u2N	II	6	B	Occ	Dunes~, Tunes~.		N
198	UR - VI	(y)u(o)R', (y)uR'	II	6	B	Occ	Cure~, De-mure~, En-dure~, I-nure~,Ob-scure, Pure~.		N
199	URN - II	u1R-n	II	6	B	Occ	Bur-nish, Gur-ney, La.bur-num, Tur-nip.		N
200	US - II	u2S1	II	6	B	Occ	Ab-struse, Ob-tuse, Ruse~.		N

Copyright © published 2022 by Adil Rehman.
www.americanaccentlearnway.com

Chapter 3:
Recognizing Vocal Patterns – Using Word List Tables.

The Word List Table provided for each Vocal Pattern will enable you to convert your pronunciation of many words at one time, rather than being limited to learning only single words at a time. Each Word List Table gives you a list of words containing a specified Vocal Pattern, enabling you to vocalize them in the American way. By practicing the Vocal Patterns in these Word List Tables you quickly shift to an American way of speaking English!

Word List Tables are provided for Vocal Patterns for which there are enough words to justify a supplementary Word List, in addition to the examples already provided with each Vocal Pattern in the Vocal Pattern Tables. Word List Tables are not provided for Vocal Patterns that have an Occasional Rate of Occurrence as there are few such words.

Word List Tables for Vocal Patterns are presented in order of: first, their Distinctiveness; second, their Rate of Occurrence; and, third, the alphanumeric order of the Vocal Pattern name. This is further explained below.

Each Word List Table begins with a "Priority-Sequence" number in the top row. Priority refers to Priority Group based on Distinctiveness and Sequence refers to the Learning Sequence number based on both Distinctiveness and Rate of Occurrence levels.

Remember, Learning Priority Group categories for Vocal Patterns have been set to correspond with their Distinctiveness categories:

Learning Priority Group 'I' corresponds with 'A', i.e. "Great" or most Distinctive Vocal Patterns;

Learning Priority Group 'II' corresponds with 'B', i.e. "Substantial" or very Distinctive Vocal Patterns; and

Learning Priority Group 'III' corresponds with 'C', i.e. "Significant" or clearly Distinctive Vocal Patterns.

Distinctiveness category 'D', i.e. "Insignificant" Distinctiveness Vocal Patterns which are nearly indistinct, are only listed in the Master Table and have not been included in the Vocal Pattern and Word List Tables.

And, the Learning Sequence categories based on both Distinctiveness and Rate of Occurrence for Vocal Patterns are:

In the Vocal Pattern Bridge Table, (in Coursebook One), '1' is for "Frequent" and '2' for "Often".

In the Vocal Pattern Inland Table, (in Coursebook Two), '4' is for "Frequent" and '5' for "Often".

In the Vocal Pattern Summit Table, (in Coursebook Three), '7' is for "Frequent" and '8" for "Often".

Word List Tables are not provided for Vocal Patterns with a Rate of Occurrence that is "Occasional", i.e. Learning Sequence category numbers '3', '6' and '9'. Learning Sequence categories, '10', '11' and '12' are associated with category 'IV', i.e. Insignificant or nearly indistinct Vocal Patterns and are not included in the Vocal Pattern or Word List Tables.

Within Priority-Sequence groups, they are in alpha-numeric order. This is illustrated below with reference to Vocal Pattern examples from the Vocal Pattern Bridge Table in Coursebook One. The Vocal Pattern Inland Table in the present Coursebook Two, and the Vocal Pattern Summit Table in Coursebook Three, follow the same order:

Vocal Pattern, AM - I (Priority-Sequence I/1), precedes Vocal Pattern, AN - I (Priority-Sequence I/1), among the Word List Tables corresponding with the "Vocal Pattern Bridge Table", because the former precedes the latter in alphanumeric order. However, Vocal Pattern, AR - II (Priority-Sequence I/1), precedes Vocal Pattern, ANK - II (Priority-Sequence I/2), though ANK - II precedes the AR - II in alphanumeric order. This is because the Rate of Occurrence for AR - II is in the higher category, i.e. "Frequent", compared with ANK - II which is in the "Often" category, as may be seen from their Priority-Sequence groups. Both 'AR - II' and 'ANK - II' are listed in the Vocal Pattern Bridge Table, which contains Vocal Patterns categorized 'I/1' and 'I/2'.

"The Vocal Pattern Bridge Table" provided in Coursebook One, "The American Accent Learnway – Cross the Bridge, Over the Divide" of this three Coursebook series, contains just over 100 Vocal Patterns. "The Vocal Pattern Inland Table" in Coursebook Two, "The American Accent Learnway – Together, On the Road Inland" contains 200 Vocal Patterns. "The Vocal Pattern Summit Table", provided in Coursebook Three, entitled "The American Accent Learnway – As One, On the Summit", contains just over 300 Vocal Patterns.

Copyright © published 2022 by Adil Rehman.
www.americanaccentlearnway.com

Tables:
Word Lists From Priority-Sequence II/4 Vocal Pattern ER - IV
Through Priority-Sequence II/5 Vocal Pattern UTT

The order of presentation is: Down the first column, down the second column, down the third column, to the first column of the next page, and so on.

Priority-Sequence: II/4		Bill
Vocal Pattern: ER - IV	Priority-Sequence: II/4	Dill
In Phonetic Script: e-*r*	Vocal Pattern: ICK - I	Drill
Example Words:	In Phonetic Script: ic*K(h), i"c*K(h)	Filled
American		Fills
Austerity	Example Words:	Fillmore
Blueberry	Brick	Frills
Burberry	Click	Gill
Cemetery	Dick	Gilt
Cleric~	Flick	Grill
Clerical	Hick	Grilled
Cranberry	Kick	Hill
Heretic	Lick	Jill
Hysterical	Nick	Jilt
Merit	Pick	Kill
Meritorious	Quick	Kilt
Merry	Sick	Milled
Peril	Slick	Phil
Serendipity	Snick	Pill
Severance	Stick	Quill
Severity	Trick	Sill
Sheriff	Wick	Skilled
Sterile		Spill
Temerity		Spilled
Territorial	Priority-Sequence: II/4	Spills
Territory	Vocal Pattern: IL - II	Still
Very	In Phonetic Script: i"l'l*, i'l'l*	Till
	Example Words:	Will

Willed
Priority-Sequence: II/4
Vocal Pattern: ING - I
In Phonetic Script: i[*ng*]1, i'[*ng*]1
Example Words:
Being
Bling
Blinking
Bring
Cling
Doing
Ending
Fling
Fling
Frying
Growing
Having
Hiring
Jogging
King
Linking
Living
Napping
Pouring
Ring
Sting
Stoking
Swing

Towing
Trying
Typing
Vying
Waiting
Wing
Yachting
Zipping
Priority-Sequence: II/4
Vocal Pattern: OO^ - I
In Phonetic Script: o2o*^, (i)o2o*^
Example Words:
Boon
Broom
Boot
Coon
Coop
Food
Fool
Goofed
Goon
Hoot
Loot
Moon
Room
Root
Scoop
Scoot

Shoot
Soon
Spool
Stooge
Stoop
Swoop
Tool
Troop
Priority-Sequence: II/5
Vocal Pattern: OT - I
In Phonetic Script: o'*T(h)*
Example Words:
Allot
Blot
Camelot
Clot
Cot
Dot
Got
Grot
Hot
Jot
Lot
Not~
Plot
Pot
Rot
Scot
Shot

Column 1	Column 2	Column 3
Slot	Example Words:	Vocal Pattern: AB - I
Snot	Brow	In Phonetic Script: a'*B*, a"*B*
Spot	Brown	Example Words:
Trot	Chowder	Cab
	Clown	Crab
	Cow	Dab
Priority-Sequence: II/5	Cowl	Drab
Vocal Pattern: OT - II	Crowd	Fab
In Phonetic Script: o'-t2*([td]), o'-t	Crown	Flab
	Dowel	Gab
Example Words:	Drown	Grab
Blotted	Flower	Jab
Blotter	Fowl	Lab
Clotted	Frown	Nab
Cotter	Glower	Slab
Grotto	How	Tab
Hotter	Howl	
Lotto	Jowl	
Motto	Now	Priority-Sequence: II/5
Otter	Owl	Vocal Pattern: AB - II
Otto	Powder	In Phonetic Script: a'B, a"B
Ottoman	Powell	Example Words:
Rotted	Power	Abs
Rotter	Row	Blabbed
Slotted	Rowdy	Cabbed
Slotting	Shower	Cabs
	Towel	Crabs
	Wow	Grabbed
Priority-Sequence: II/5		Grabs
Vocal Pattern: OW - I		Jabbed
In Phonetic Script: o*(a)'w	Priority-Sequence: II/5	Jabs

Nabs	Example Words:	Bagged
Nabbed	Bagged	Dagger
Scabs	Bags	Flagging
Slabbed	Crags	Laggard
Slabs	Drags	Lagging
Stabbed	Flagged	Maggie
Stabs	Flags	Maggot
Tabs	Lagged	Ragged~
	Magnet	Ragging
	Nagged	Sagging
Priority-Sequence: II/5	Pragmatic	Shaggy
Vocal Pattern: AG - I	Quagmire	Staggered
In Phonetic Script: *a'G1(h)*	Ragged~	Wagon
Example Words:	Rags	
Bag	Sagged	
Brag	Sags	Priority-Sequence: II/5
Crag	Snagged	Vocal Pattern: AIR - I
Drag	Snags	In Phonetic Script: a*i*(e)'*R*'
Flag	Stags	
Gag	Tagged	Example Words:
Lag	Tags	Air
Nag	Wagged	Blair
Snag	Wags	Chair
Stag		Chairman
Tag		Claire
Wag	Priority-Sequence: II/5	Fair
	Vocal Pattern: AG - III	Flair
	In Phonetic Script: a'-*g1*, a-*g1*	Hair
Priority-Sequence: II/5	Example Words:	Lair
Vocal Pattern: AG - II	Agate	Pair
In Phonetic Script: a'G1	Baggage	Stair

Priority-Sequence: II/5
Vocal Pattern: AIR - II
In Phonetic Script: a*i*(e)'R', a*i*(e)'R
Example Words:
Affairs
Aired
Airs
Chaired
Chairman
Chairs
Flairs
Lairs
Paired
Stairs

Priority-Sequence: II/5
Vocal Pattern: AL - I
In Phonetic Script: a*(o)'L'
Example Words:
All
Alter
Appalled
Bald
Ball
Baltic
Call
Called

Enthralled
Fall
Falls
Falter
Galled
Gibraltar
Halls
Halted
Halter
Mall
Malt
Salted
Scald
Stalled
Stalls
Tall
Walden
Wall
Walls
Walter

Priority-Sequence: II/5
Vocal Pattern: AL - II
In Phonetic Script: a*(o)-l
Example Words:
Appalling
Caller
Calling
Falling
Galling

Installer
Installing
Smaller
Smallish
Stalling
Swallow
Swallows
Wallow
Wallowed
Wallowing

Priority-Sequence: II/5
Vocal Pattern: AM - II
In Phonetic Script: a"-*m*, a'-*m*
Example Words:
Amateur
Calamity
Calamitous
Camel
Camera
Contaminate
Contaminant
Cramming
Famine
Glamorous
Grammar
Hammer
Inflammable
Inflammable
Jamming

Laminate
Parameter
Ramming
Ramification
Shamming
Slammer
Slamming
Stamina
Stammer
Trammel
Priority-Sequence: II/5
Vocal Pattern: AM - III
In Phonetic Script: a"M, a'M
Example Words:
Ample
Amplify
Camped
Champ
Crammed
Example
Lamp
Ram
Rammed
Sam
Sample
Scammed
Scramble
Sham
Slam

Slammed
Stamp
Tramp
Trample
Priority-Sequence: II/5
Vocal Pattern: AN - III
In Phonetic Script: a"N, a'N
Example Words:
Angela
Los Angeles
Atlantic
Brandy
Branded
Canada
Candid
Candor
Candy
Frantic
Mandatory
Pandora
Phantom
Semantic
Slander
Standard
Tangent
Tangerine
Tangential
Veranda

Priority-Sequence: II/5
Vocal Pattern: AN - IV
In Phonetic Script: a'-N, a-N
Example Words:
Analogue
Animal
Anna
Annotate
Banner
Banning
Bannister
Canada
Canister
Cannery
Canny
Canopy
Flannel
Granite
Hannah
Janet
Manager
Manifold
Manners
Panacea
Panel
Panic
Pannier
Panning
Panoply
Planet

Sanitation

Sanity

Spanish

Tanning

Priority-Sequence: II/5

Vocal Pattern: ANC - I

In Phonetic Script: a"nc*($S1$), a'nc*($S1$)

Example Words:

Chance

Dance

Enhance

Finance

France

Glance

Lance

Prance

Romance

Stance

Trance

Priority-Sequence: II/5

Vocal Pattern: ANC - III

In Phonetic Script: a"N-c*($s1$), a'N-c*($s1$)

Example Words:

Cancel

Cancer

Chances

Chancy

Dancer

Dancing

Emancipation

Enhances

Fancy

Finances

Glances

Glancing

Lancers

Nancy

Prances

Prancing

Romances

Stances

Trances

Priority-Sequence: II/5

Vocal Pattern: AND - II

In Phonetic Script: a'N-D, a'N-D

Example Words:

Abandon

Banded

Branding

Candid

Candle

Candor

Clandestine

Dandelion

Expanding

Grandest

Handed

Handle

Landed

Landing

Mandarin

Mandatory

Panda

Pander

Random

Rwanda

Sandal

Sanding

Slander

Spandex

Veranda

Priority-Sequence: II/5

Vocal Pattern: ANG - I

In Phonetic Script: a'[ng1]-($g1$)

Example Words:

Anger

Angle

Angry

Angular

Angus

Bangle

Dangle

Hanger	
Haranguer	
Jangle	
Kangaroo	
Languor	
Mangle	
Mango	
New Fangled	
Orangutan	
Spangled	
Tangle	
Tango	
Triangle	
Triangulate	
Wangle	
Wrangle	
Priority-Sequence: II/5	
Vocal Pattern: ANG - II	
In Phonetic Script: a'[ng1]	
Example Words:	
Bang	
Bangs	
Banged	
Clang	
Clanged	
Fang	
Fangs	
Hang	
Hanged	

Harangue	
Pang	
Rang	
Sang	
Slang	
Sprang	
Tang	
Priority-Sequence: II/5	
Vocal Pattern: ANT - IV	
In Phonetic Script: aN-T, a"N-T	
Example Words:	
Antic	
Atlantic	
Banter	
Canter	
Frantic	
Granted	
Granter	
Granting	
Lantern	
Mantel	
Panting	
Pantry	
Planter	
Ranted	
Ranting	
Romantic	
Semantic	

Shanty	
Slanted	
Substantive~	
Priority-Sequence: II/5	
Vocal Pattern: AP - II	
In Phonetic Script: a' P	
Example Words:	
Adapt	
Adaptation	
Apps	
Caps	
Clapped	
Collapse	
Elapse	
Flapped	
Flaps	
Gaps	
Maps	
Perhaps	
Rapt	
Relapse	
Sapped	
Snaps	
Strapped	
Synapse	
Tapped	
Taps	
Trapped	
Zapped	

Priority-Sequence: II/5	
Vocal Pattern: AP - III	
In Phonetic Script: a'-P, a-"P	
Example Words:	
Apparatus	
Apparition	
Appetite	
Apple	
Capital	
Capping	
Dapple	
Flapping	
Happen	
Happening	
Happy	
Lapping	
Napping	
Rapid	
Rapping	
Snapper	
Snapping	
Strapping	
Tappet	
Tapping	
Trapping	
Vapid	
Priority-Sequence: II/5	

Vocal Pattern: AR - V
In Phonetic Script: a*(e)-*r*
Example Words:
Arid
Adversary
Apparel
Aquarium
Arrow
Aviary
Barium
Baron
Barracuda
Barrel
Barren
Barry
Canary
Cara
Caret
Carrie
Carrot
Carry
Carried
Daring
Dictionary
February
Fiduciary
Garish
Gary
Guarantee
Harry
Hereditary

Incendiary
January
Judiciary
Larry
Larynx
Library
Mariner~
Marry
Mary
Military
Obituary
Parents
Paris
Parish
Parity
Pecuniary
Pharaoh~
Sarah
Seminary
Sharing
Sharon
Topiary
Tributary
Various
Priority-Sequence: II/5
Vocal Pattern: AS - IV
In Phonetic Script: a'-*s*1
Example Words:
Ascertain

Asinine	Elastic	Rattle
Castle	Faster	Seattle
Classic	Fastidious	Smattering
Classical	Fasting	Splatter
Exasperate	Gastronomic	Shatter
Fascinate	Lasting	Tatter
Fasten	Master	Tattle
Hassle	Masticate	
Massacre	Metastasize	
Massif	Nasty	Priority-Sequence: II/5
Massive	Pastel	Vocal Pattern: AT - IV
Passing	Plaster	In Phonetic Script: A-t2*([td]), A-t
Passive	Plastic	
Tassel	Procrastinate	Example Words:
Vassal		Abated
		Allocated
	Priority-Sequence: II/5	Assimilated
Priority-Sequence: II/5	Vocal Pattern: AT - III	Belated
Vocal Pattern: AST – II	In Phonetic Script: a-t2*([td])t*, a-tt*	Cater
In Phonetic Script: a'S1-*t*		Collated
Example Words:	Example Words:	Conflating
Asterisk	Batter	Crated
Aston	Battery	Crater
Astronaut	Battle	Deflated
Astronomic	Cattle	Elated
Blasting	Flattered	Gated
Castanet	Latter	Grated
Castaway	Matter	Inflated
Casting	Natter	Later
Dastard	Patter	Pater
Drastic	Prattle	Potato~

Column 1

Rated
Related
Relating
Rotated
Sated
Stated
Priority-Sequence: II/5
Vocal Pattern: AU^ - I
In Phonetic Script: a*u*(o)'-^, a*u*(o)(w)-^
Example Words:
Audio
Audition
Authentic
Author
Authority
Auto
Cauterize
Claudine
Daughter
Haughty
Laura
Raucous
Saute
Slaughter
Priority-Sequence: II/5
Vocal Pattern: AU^ - II

Column 2

In Phonetic Script: a*(o)'u*^ a*(o)u*(w)^
Example Words:
Applaud
Caught
Caulk
Cause
Clause
Distraught
Flaunt
Fraught
Gaunt
Gauntlet
Hauled
Laud
Maude
Mauled
Mauve
Naught
Paul
Pause
Saul
Saunter
Staunch
Taught
Taunt
Taut
Priority-Sequence: II/5
Vocal Pattern: AU^ - III

Column 3

In Phonetic Script: a*(o)'u*-^, a*(o)u*(w)-^
Example Words:
Applauded
Applauding
Cauliflower
Causation
Causing
Causing
Cauterize
Caution
Daughter
Fauna
Hauling
Lauded
Lauding
Nausea
Pausing
Sauna
Saute
Slaughter
Priority-Sequence: II/5
Vocal Pattern: AW
In Phonetic Script: a*(o)w
Example Words:
Awe
Awesome
Awful
Bawdy

Bawl
Brawl
Claw
Coleslaw
Crawfish
Draw
Fawn
Flaw
Flawed
Hawk
Jaw
Lawman
Lawn
Lawyer
Paw
Raw
Saw
Spawn
Tawdry
Tawny
Trawler
Priority-Sequence: II/5
Vocal Pattern: ED - III
In Phonetic Script: E'D, ED
Example Words:
Buried
Carried
Curried
Hurried

Married
Parried
Scurried
Tarried
Worried
Priority-Sequence: II/5
Vocal Pattern: EN - III
In Phonetic Script: e"N, e'N
Example Words:
Amended
Appended
Apprehended
Befriended
Bending
Cemented
Depending
Distended
Extended
Ending
Fended
Horrendous
Intended
Lending
Mended
Mending
Pending
Relented
Rented
Renting

Reprehensible
Sending
Scented
Splendid
Talented
Tending
Trending
Unattended
Unrelenting
Wended
Wending
Priority-Sequence: II/5
Vocal Pattern: ENT - II
In Phonetic Script: e*n*, e-*n*
Example Words:
Center
Consented
Dissenting
Dented
Enter
Incidental
Plenty
Presentable
Preventable
Rental
Renter
Rented
Resented
Sentimental

Priority-Sequence: II/5
Vocal Pattern: END - I
In Phonetic Script: *e'nD(h)*, *e''nD(h)*

Example Words:
Amend
Ascend
Bend
Blend
Defend
Depend
End
Extend
Fend
Friend
Friendly
Intend
Lend
Pend
Pretend
Rend
Send
Tend
Trend
Wend

Priority-Sequence: II/5
Vocal Pattern: ENT - I
In Phonetic Script: *e'nT(h)*, *e''nT(h)*

Example Words:
Ascent
Assent
Bent
Cement
Dent
Descent
Dissent
Lent
Present
Prevent
Relent
Sent
Spent
Resent
Stent
Tent
Went

Priority-Sequence: II/5
Vocal Pattern: ENT - II
In Phonetic Script: e*n*-t2*([td]), e-*n*t*

Example Words:
Center
Consented
Dissenting
Demented
Dented
Enter

Entered
Entering
Incidental
Mentor
Mentored
Plenty
Presentable
Preventable
Rental
Renter
Rented
Resented
Sentimental
Tentacle
Unrelenting

Priority-Sequence: II/5
Vocal Pattern: ER - V
In Phonetic Script: e1R

Example Words:
Certain
Certify
Cervical
Cervix
Commercial
Determine
Diverge
Divergent
Diverges
Emergency

Column 1	Column 2	Column 3
Emerge	Stern	
Emergent	Sternly	
Emerges	Tern	Priority-Sequence: II/5
Emerging	Western	Vocal Pattern: ET - II
Energetic		In Phonetic Script: e-t2*([td]), e-*t*
Energy		
Ermine	Priority-Sequence: II/5	Example Words:
Merge	Vocal Pattern: ERN - II	Aesthetic
Merger	In Phonetic Script: e1R'-*n*	Alphabetical
Merges	Example Words:	Antithetical
Merlin	Alternate	Ascetic
Revert	Concerning	Better
Sterling	Ernest	Betting
Verge	Eternal	Confetti
Verges	External	Cosmetic
Verging	Governance	Empathetic
Version	Infernal	Etcetera
Vertical	Internal	Fetter
	Internet	Fretting
	Fraternal	Getting
Priority-Sequence: II/5	Fraternity	Heterogeneous
Vocal Pattern: ERN - I	Kernel	Inveterate
In Phonetic Script: e1RN	Maternal	Jetting
Example Words:	Maternity	Letter
Eastern	Modernization	Pathetic
Ferns	Paternal	Petting
Govern	Paternity	Prophetic
Lectern	Tabernacle	Rhetoric
Modern	Vernacular	Setter
Northern	Vernal	Setting
Southern	Westernization	Sympathetic

Veteran

Priority-Sequence: II/5

Vocal Pattern: ET - III

In Phonetic Script: E'-t2*([td]), E'-*t*

Example Words:

- Competed
- Competing
- Deleted
- Fetal
- Greeter
- Greeting
- Meted
- Meter
- Peter
- Sheeting
- Teeter

Priority-Sequence: II/5

Vocal Pattern: ETT

In Phonetic Script: e-t2*([td])t*

Example Words:

- Better
- Betting
- Fetter
- Getting
- Fetters
- Kettle

Letter

- Letting
- Nettle
- Petted
- Petting
- Setter
- Setting
- Settle
- Settled
- Settling
- Vetted
- Vetting
- Wetting

Priority-Sequence: II/5

Vocal Pattern: EW^ - I

In Phonetic Script: e*(i)(u2)w^, e*(u2)'w^

Example Words:

- Brewed
- Chew
- Chewed
- Chews
- Crew
- Crewed
- Crews
- Dew
- Drew
- Flew
- Grew

Lewd

- News~
- Screw
- Screws
- Stew~
- Stewed~
- Strewn

Priority-Sequence: II/5

Vocal Pattern: EW^ - II

In Phonetic Script: e*(i)(u2)-*w*, e*(u2)'-*w*

Example Words:

- Brewery
- Brewing
- Chewing
- Crewing
- Leeward
- Renewal
- Renewing
- Sinewy
- Steward
- Stewing

Priority-Sequence: II/5

Vocal Pattern: IBUT - II

In Phonetic Script: i-bU-t*(d)

Example Words:

- Attributed

Column 1	Column 2	Column 3
Attributing	Relief	Mighty
Contributed	Relieve	Nightingale
Contributing	Sallied	Sighting
Contributor	Siege	Slight
Distributed	Storied	Slighted
Distributing	Stories	Tighten
Distributor	Studied	
	Sullied	
	Tallied	Priority-Sequence: II/5
Priority-Sequence: II/5	Tarried	Vocal Pattern: IL - III
Vocal Pattern: IE^ - I	Varied	In Phonetic Script: I'L', I(a1)L'
In Phonetic Script: i*E'^	Wearied	
Example Words:	Worried	Example Words:
Belief		Bile
Believe		Defile
Bullied	Priority-Sequence: II/5	Exile
Bullies	Vocal Pattern: IGHT - I	File
Buried	In Phonetic Script: I'g*h*-t2*([td]), I'g*h*-t	Guile
Carried	Example Words:	Mile
Curried	Brighten	Nile
Frieze	Brighter	Pile
Grief	Enlighten	Revile
Grieve	Fighting	Rile
Harried	Flighty	Riled
Hurried	Frighten	Senile
Lien~	Frightening	Sterile
Married	Heighten	Smile
Muddied	Knighted	Tile
Parried	Lighting	While
Queried	Mightier	
Rallied		

Priority-Sequence: II/5
Vocal Pattern: IM - II
In Phonetic Script: I'M, (a2)IM
Example Words:
Chime
Climb
Climbed
Climbs
Crimes
Dime
Dimes
Grime
Lime
Mime
Pantomime
Prime
Slime
Time
Timed
Times

Priority-Sequence: II/5
Vocal Pattern: IN - II
In Phonetic Script: I'N, (a2)IN
Example Words:
Asinine
Bind
Bind
Blinds
Decline

Dined
Divine
Feline
Find
Fined
Grind
Histamine
Incline
Kind
Line
Melamine
Mind
Nine
Opine
Opined
Pines
Pint
Remind
Rind
Saline
Wind~
Wines

Priority-Sequence: II/5
Vocal Pattern: IR - I
In Phonetic Script: I(a1)R', I'R
Example Words:
Admire
Aspire
Attire

Desired
Dire
Empire
Entire
Expire
Fire
Hire
Inquire
Inspire
Ire
Ireland~
Mire
Respire
Retire
Spire
Tire
Wire

Priority-Sequence: II/5
Vocal Pattern: IR - II
In Phonetic Script: I(a1)R, I'R
Example Words:
Admires
Aspired
Attires
Desired
Empire
Entire
Expired
Fires

Hired
Inquires
Inspires
Ireland~
Mired
Respires
Retired
Spires
Tires
Wired
Priority-Sequence: II/5
Vocal Pattern: IR - III
In Phonetic Script: i1R
Example Words:
Bird
Circle
Dirge
Dirt
Fir
First
Gird
Girl
Irk
Sir
Sirloin
Skirmish
Skirt
Squirm
Squirt

Stir
Whirl
Priority-Sequence: II/5
Vocal Pattern: IS - II
In Phonetic Script: i"S1, i'S1
Example Words:
Assist
Brisk
Crisp
Disc
Exist
Fist
Frisk
Gist
Grist
Insist
Lisp
List
Mist
Resist
Twist
Whisk
Wistful
Wrist
Priority-Sequence: II/5
Vocal Pattern: OC - I
In Phonetic Script: o'C(h)

Example Words:
Block
Clock
Cock
Dock
Flock
Frock
Hock
Knock
Lock
Mock
Rock
Shock
Smock
Stock
Stock
Unlock
Priority-Sequence: II/5
Vocal Pattern: OC - II
In Phonetic Script: o'C
Example Words:
Blocked
Clocks
Clocked
Docks
Doctor
Flocked
Flocks
Frocks

Hocks
Knocks
Locked
Mocks
Mocked
Octagon
October
Octopus
Rocked
Rocks
Shocked
Shocks
Smocks
Socks
Stocked
Stocks
Unlocked

Priority-Sequence: II/5
Vocal Pattern: OC - III
In Phonetic Script: o'-*c*, o'-C
Example Words:

Blocking
Crocodile
Docket
Flocking
Knocking
Locker
Locket
Locking

Moccasin
Mocking
Rocker
Rocket
Rocking
Shocking
Soccer
Sprocket
Stocking

Priority-Sequence: II/5
Vocal Pattern: OD - III
In Phonetic Script: o'-D
Example Words:

Body
Coddle
Coddling
Codification
Codify
Fodder
Model
Modeling
Modern
Modernity
Modest
Modesty
Modicum
Modification
Modify
Nodding

Nodded
Plodding
Shoddy

Priority-Sequence: II/5
Vocal Pattern: OG - I
In Phonetic Script: o'*G*
Example Words:

Analog / Analogue
Blog
Bog
Catalog / Catalogue
Clog
Cog
Demagogue
Flog
Fog
Frog
Hog
Prologue
Slog
Travelogue

Priority-Sequence: II/5
Vocal Pattern: OG - II
In Phonetic Script: o'G
Example Words:

Analogs /Analogues
Blogged

Blogs	Toggle	Frolic
Cataloged	Toggling	Holiday
Catalogs		Hollow
Clogs		Jollity
Cogs	Priority-Sequence: II/5	Jolly
Demagogues	Vocal Pattern: OG - IV	Lollypop
Dogged	In Phonetic Script: o'-g2*(j)	Molecule
Flogged	Example Words:	Molly
Frogs	Cogitate	Policy
Hogged	Homogenize	Polish
Hogs	Homogeny	Politics
Logs	Logic	Pollen
Slogged	Logical	Rollicking
Slogs	Misogyny	Scholar
Travelogues	Pedagogical	Solace
	Pedagogy~	Solemn
	Progeny	Solid
Priority-Sequence: II/5	Roger	
Vocal Pattern: OG - III		
In Phonetic Script: o'-G, o'-g		Priority-Sequence: II/5
	Priority-Sequence: II/5	Vocal Pattern: OM - II
Example Words:	Vocal Pattern: OL - II	In Phonetic Script: o'-m
Blogger	In Phonetic Script: o'-l, o'-l	Example Words:
Blogging	Example Words:	Abominable
Boggle	Abolish	Abomination
Hogging	Colic	Anomaly
Leap Frogging	College	Astronomic
Logger	Dollop	Atomic
Logging	Follow	Comedy
Slogger	Follow	Comet
Slogging	Folly	Comic

Comma
Comment
Commentate
Commerce
Common
Dominant
Dominate
Economical
Economize
Economy
Ergonomic
Grommet
Hominid
Ignominy
Nomenclature
Nominal
Nominate
Nomination
Omelet
Ominous
Promenade
Prominent
Promise
Promulgate
Tommy
Priority-Sequence: II/5
Vocal Pattern: ON - III
In Phonetic Script: o)'*N*, o*N*'
Example Words:

Aileron
Freon
Gone~
Ion
Jon~
Neon
On~
Ron~
Salon
Shone
Priority-Sequence: II/5
Vocal Pattern: ON - IV
In Phonetic Script: o'N
Example Words:
Abscond
Blond
Concave
Condominium
Condor
Console~
Contact
Contents
Contest
Context
Contrary
Convex
Fronds
Montreal
Monster

Orthodontics
Pontiff
Pontoon
Pronto
Rhonda
Tonsil
Toronto
Priority-Sequence: II/5
Vocal Pattern: ON - V
In Phonetic Script: o'-*n*
Example Words:
Anonymous
Astonish
Bonny
Conifer
Economy
Eponymous
Iconic
Histrionic
Honest
Honesty
Honorable
McDonald
Mnemonic
Monetary
Monument
Ronald
Ronnie
Sonic

Sonnet
Tonic
Veronica
Priority-Sequence: II/5
Vocal Pattern: ONG - I
In Phonetic Script: o)'[ng], o[ng]
Example Words:
Along
Belong
Belongs
Furlong
Hong Kong
Long
Prolong
Prongs
Sarong
Song
Strong
Stronghold
Throng
Tong
Tongs
Priority-Sequence: II/5
Vocal Pattern: OO^ - II
In Phonetic Script: O2o*-^, (i)o2o*-^

Example Words:
Blooming
Booted
Booting
Brooding
Gloomy
Hooted
Looted
Looter
Moody
Mooning
Mooted
Noodle
Noodles
Oozing
Roomy
Rooted
Rooting
Schooner
Scooter
Shooting
Smoother
Snooty
Sooner
Soothing
Spooning
Swooning
Tooted
Tooting

Priority-Sequence: II/5
Vocal Pattern: OP - I
In Phonetic Script: o'P(h)
Example Words:
Cop
Crop
Drop
Flop
Hop
Lop
Mop
Plop
Pop
Prop
Shop
Slop
Sop
Stop
Top
Priority-Sequence: II/5
Vocal Pattern: OP - II
In Phonetic Script: o'P
Example Words:
Cropped
Crops
Dropped
Flops
Hops
Lopped

Mopped
Plops
Pops
Propped
Shopped
Sop
Stopped
Stops
Topped
Priority-Sequence: II/5
Vocal Pattern: OP - III
In Phonetic Script: o'-P
Example Words:
Dropping
Hopping
Microscopic
Mopping
Operate
Operation
Opposite
Opposition
Optical
Popular
Populate
Population
Properly
Property
Shopper
Sloppy

Stopping
Topic
Topic
Topical
Tropic
Tropical
Tropics
Priority-Sequence: II/5
Vocal Pattern: ORR - I
In Phonetic Script: o)'-*rr**, o-*rr**
Example Words:
Correspondent
Horrendous
Horrid
Horrible
Horrific
Horror
Lorry
Norris
Porridge
Sorry
Tomorrow
Torrent
Torrential
Torrid
Note: All of the above examples also apply to ORR – II, phonetically Scripted: o'-*rr**. However, ORR – I could

be the more popular of the two. Example Words exclusively associated with ORR – II are listed in the Vocal Pattern Inland Table.

Priority-Sequence: II/5
Vocal Pattern: OS - I
In Phonetic Script: o'*S*
Example Words:
Cosby
Costume
Foster
Hospice
Hospital
Hostel
Jostle
Los Angeles
Moscow
Nostalgia
Ostensible
Ostentatious
Ostrich
Posthumous~
Prosthetic
Priority-Sequence: II/5
Vocal Pattern: OS - II
In Phonetic Script: o'-s*s
Example Words:

Bossing
Bossy
Crosses
Crossing
Flosses
Flossing
Losses
Mossy
Ossify
Posse
Possible
Tosses
Tossing

Priority-Sequence: II/5
Vocal Pattern: UA^ - I
In Phonetic Script: u*(W)a*(o)^
Example Words:
Guava
Qualify
Quality
Squad
Squall
Squalid
Squander
Squat
Squatter
Suave

Priority-Sequence: II/5
Vocal Pattern: UN - II
In Phonetic Script: u1N
Example Words:
Asunder
Blunder
Blunted
Bundle
Bunting
Crunches
Grunted
Grunting
Hunted
Hunter
Hunting
Luncheon
Lunches
Munching
Punches
Punching
Punted
Punting
Shunted
Stunted
Sunday
Thunder
Truncheon
Trundle
Under

Priority-Sequence: II/5
Vocal Pattern: UR - II
In Phonetic Script: u1R', u1R
Example Words:
Adventure
Annexure
Azure
Blur
Censure
Denture
Lecture
Occur
Purr
Slur
Spur
Sure

Priority-Sequence: II/5
Vocal Pattern: UR - III
In Phonetic Script: u1R
Example Words:
Blurred
Burn
Curl
Curtail
Furled
Furtive
Nasturtium
Occurred

Sturdy
Surly
Unfurl
Priority-Sequence: II/5
Vocal Pattern: UR - V
In Phonetic Script: u1-*r*
Example Words:
Bury
Buried
Canterbury
Century
Current
Curry
Flurry
Furry
Hurried
Hurry
Scurrilous
Scurry
Priority-Sequence: II/5
Vocal Pattern: US - I
In Phonetic Script: u2-s3*([*zh*])
Example Words:
Collusion
Conclusion
Contusion

Delusion
Exclusion
Extrusion
Illusion
Inclusion
Intrusion
Seclusion
Priority-Sequence: II/5
Vocal Pattern: UT - I
In Phonetic Script: U-t2*([td]), U-t
Example Words:
Computed
Computer
Computing
Contributed
Contributing
Contributor
Disputing
Distributed
Distributing
Distributor
Electrocuted
Executed
Executing
Executor~
Mutant
Muted
Muting

Refuted
Refuting
Priority-Sequence: II/5
Vocal Pattern: UT - II
In Phonetic Script: u1-t2*([td])t*
Example Words:
Butted
Butter
Buttering
Button
Button
Clutter
Cluttered
Cluttering
Cutter
Cutting
Flutter
Glutted
Gutted
Gutter
Mutter
Muttered
Putty
Rebuttal
Shutter
Shutting
Strutted
Stutter

Priority-Sequence: II/5
Vocal Pattern: UTT
u1-t2*([td]), u1-t
Example Words:
Butted
Butter
Clutter
Cutting
Fluttered
Gutter
Mutter
Putted
Putter
Putting~
Shutter
Stutter
Stuttering

Copyright © published 2022 by Adil Rehman.
www.americanaccentlearnway.com

Chapter 4:
Moving Ahead, From Here.

The Vocal Pattern Summit Table is in the final of this three Coursebook series, entitled "Speaking the American Way – As One, on the Summit". It contains just over 300 clearly Distinctive Vocal Patterns. Not being among the more Distinctive of Vocal Patterns, it is likely that many of these may have escaped the notice of learners. Here too, you can self-diagnose the Vocal Patterns you need to change. When these are learned, any significant gaps that remain in how Vocal Patterns are vocalized are closed.

The following Table contains 10 Vocal Patterns from the Vocal Pattern Summit Table. You can see which of these you vocalize differently than Americans. You can compare the levels of Distinctiveness of Vocal Patterns across the different categories, i.e Great (i.e. most Distinctive) in the Vocal Pattern Bridge Table presented in Coursebook One, Substantial (i.e. very Distinctive) in the Vocal Pattern Inland Table presented in Coursebook Two, and Significant (i.e. clearly Distinctive) illustrated in the Table below, noting how Distinctiveness decreases across the levels. The Table indicates the extent of difference between the American Accent and the British and reveals the details of vocalization in the American Accent. Armed with Coursebooks Two and Three with the Vocal Pattern Inland and Summit Tables, in addition to Coursebook One with the Vocal Pattern Bridge Table, you will be able to look up words from a comprehensive listing of Distinctive Vocal Patterns in spoken American English, observe how each is vocalized, and close the remaining gap between the way you speak and the American way of speaking.

Note: Over 840 Vocal Patterns have been identified and categorized. These constitute the Vocal Pattern Master Table. Only after compilation of the Vocal Pattern Master Table was done, was it possible to identify the Vocal Pattern Bridge, Inland and Summit Tables.

The Vocal Pattern Master Table also identifies Vocal Patterns categorized as "Insignificant" in terms of their Distinctiveness, i.e. those that are nearly Indistinct.

The Vocal Pattern Tables contain a comprehensive listing of Distinctive Vocal Patterns across the English Language and show how they are vocalized in the American Accent. Longer Vocal Patterns are represented by shorter Vocal Patterns or by a Vocal Pattern family.

The Vocal Pattern Master Table, the Vocal Pattern Bridge Table, the Vocal Pattern Inland Table and the Vocal Pattern Summit Table are proprietary intellectual property.© All rights reserved.

Table:
Looking Ahead At A Few Vocal Patterns From
The Vocal Pattern Summit Table

Columns									
1	2	3	4	5	6	7	8	9	10
Serial	Vocal Pattern Name	Vocal Pattern Vocalization	LP	LS	ApDE	RoOE	Word Example with Vocal Pattern (Pauses shown)	Change OK/C	Word List Table Y/N
315	AG - VI	A'g2*(*J*) (*h*)e*	III	8	C	Oft	Cage, Page, Sage, Stage, Wage.		Y
347	EB - I	e-B	III	8	C	Oft	E-bbing, E-bo-ny, Ce-le-bri-ty, Re-bel, Tre-ble, We-bbing.		Y
392	ICK - II	i-c1**k*	III	8	C	Oft	Cri-cket, Fli-cker, Sti-cker, Stri-cken, Wi-cked, Wi-cker.		Y
419	IR - VII	i-r	III	8	C	Oft	Mi.ra-cle, Mi-rage, In-qui.ry~, Spi.rit, I-ri.di-scent.		Y
460	OT - IV	O'-t3*([sh]), (a1)O-t3*([sh])	III	8	C	Oft	E-mo-tio-nal, Lo-tion, Mo-tion, No-tio-n, Po-tion, Quo-tient.		Y
509	UP - II	u1-P	III	8	C	Oft	Mu-ppet, Pu-ppet, Pu-ppy, Stu-per~, Stu-pid~, Su-pper, Su-pple, Su-preme.		Y
541	AST - III	a1-*s*1t	III	9	C	Occ	A-sto-nish, A-stride, A-stig-ma.tism, A-stute.		N
593	UNG - IV	u1N-g2*(*j*), uN-g2*(*j*)	III	9	C	Occ	Dun-geon, Pun-gent, Plun-ging, Ex-pun-ges.		N

Copyright © published 2022 by Adil Rehman.
www.americanaccentlearnway.com

About the Author

It is relevant to share a bit about my own language development, my education and career – the context that led me to devote myself full-time, for many years, to the creation of this Course.

I grew up in India where I went through most of my education. Though my parents came from different language backgrounds, the language spoken at home was English. My mother learned English at a Convent School in Bombay from Irish teachers. My father qualified at Cambridge University in the United Kingdom, becoming, in his career, the Legal Director for a multi-national organization, and later, the Principal of a Law College. Other influences included schooling at British schools for expatriates in India and subsequent schooling in the Indian Public School system.

My mind was opened to the subject of Linguistics while at college. After a Bachelor's degree in English & Psychology, and then, a Master's degree in Sociology, both from Bombay University, I went on to have a career in Human Resource Management & Consulting with well known companies in India, the Middle East and the United States.

I continued my education, along with my profession. In India, my learning from a two year foundation course for a doctoral level program in Human Resource Development contributed greatly to the scientific approach underlying the development of the American Accent Learnway™. After moving to the United States in 2003, I earned a Master of Science Degree in Human Resource Management from Golden Gate University, in San Francisco.

Over the course of my life, exposure to the diverse Accents of English across the world, the phonetics of other languages, and subsequently, to the English spoken in America, also provided relevant background for this work.

I see that the present work called upon all that I have learned as a student in the areas of Human sciences and Language, and as a Human Resource Development professional. It required learning about what is knowledge, – and how to create it. The excitement of this pursuit was also important. From the beginning, I saw the purpose as bold. It was actually a much bigger adventure than I anticipated, with many unknowns to consider along the way. What has been most personally satisfying is that it all conforms with fact.

I believe it will be useful for many people. I am keen that everyone who is interested in speaking the American way see what has been learned. For me, both the journey and what it revealed has been fascinating.

All Rights Reserved. Copyright © published 2022 by Adil Rehman. For contact and other information, please see the website: www.americanaccentlearnway.com

www.ingramcontent.com/pod-product-compliance
Lightning Source LLC
Chambersburg PA
CBHW080856120626

46553CB00009B/2647